Upcycled Gifts and Gadgets

Anastasia Suen

Rourke
Educational Media

rourkeeducationalmedia.com

SUPPLIES TO COMPLETE ALL PROJECTS:

- CD
- CD cases (standard size)
- clipboard (optional)
- colored tissue paper
- decorative paper
- ear buds
- electronic device (cell phone or MP3 player)
- glue
- glue stick
- hot glue gun (adult permission)
- keyboard
- LED tea lights
- magazines
- markers
- newspaper or cardboard
- paint
- paper
- paper cups (used, rinsed and dried)
- paper tube (from toilet paper and paper towels)
- pencil
- photos
- picture frame
- plastic grocery bags
- plastic spoons
- pushpins
- ruler
- safety goggles
- scissors
- screwdriver (flathead)
- small glass jar
- spray paint
- stickers
- stick-on letters
- tape (clear)
- tape (colored)
- toothpicks
- tracing paper
- washi tape
- X-Acto knife (for adult use only)

Table of Contents

Upcycled Gifts and Gadgets **5**

Paper Cup Speakers. **6**

Plastic Bag Bracelet **10**

CD Photo Cube **14**

Keyboard Letter Frame. **18**

Plastic Spoon Flower Light. **24**

Glossary **30**

Index. **31**

Show What You Know. **31**

Further Reading. **31**

About the Author **32**

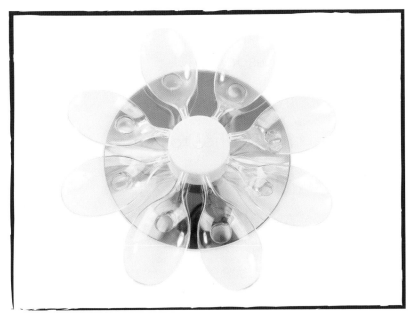

Upcycled Gifts and Gadgets

Use something old to make something new and even better.

Are you ready to **upcycle**? Make music speakers from paper cups. Braid a plastic bag into a bracelet. Twist and turn old CD cases into a photo cube. Transform an old keyboard into art. Add plastic spoons to an old CD and create a shiny flower light!

Paper Cup Speakers

- used paper cups, rinsed and dried

- pencil

- scissors

- X-Acto knife (for adult use only)

- pushpins

- paper tube (from toilet paper and paper towels)

- toothpicks

- electronic device (cell phone or MP3 player)

- decorations such as paint, stickers, or colored tape (optional)

Tip:
Rinse the paper cups with hot water before you reuse them to make your speakers.

THREE WAYS TO MAKE A MUSICAL GADGET!

Here's How:

Use one cup with pushpins:

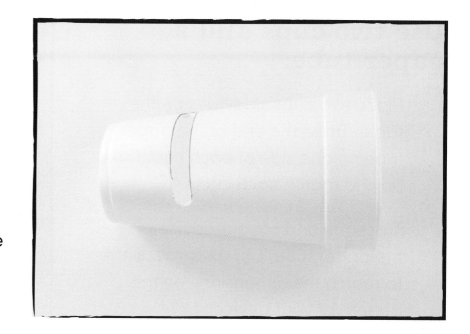

1. Trace the end of your device near the bottom of a paper cup.

2. Cut a narrow slit to match the bottom **dimensions** of your device.

3. Press a pushpin into each side of the cup to hold it in place.

4. Place your device into the slit and listen to the music!

Tip:
If you need help cutting the narrow opening, ask an adult to cut it for you with an X-Acto knife.

Use two cups and a paper tube:

1. Place two cups sideways on the table. Trace the end of the paper tube on one side of each cup. Cut a hole to match each circle.

2. Trace the end of your device on the paper tube. Cut a narrow slit to match the dimensions on the bottom of your device.

3. Place one end of the tube into each cup. Then place your device into the slit and press play.

Tip:
Decorate the paper tube and the paper cups after you cut the openings. You can paint the paper, wrap it with colored tape, or add stickers.

Use four cups, two toothpicks, and your ear buds:

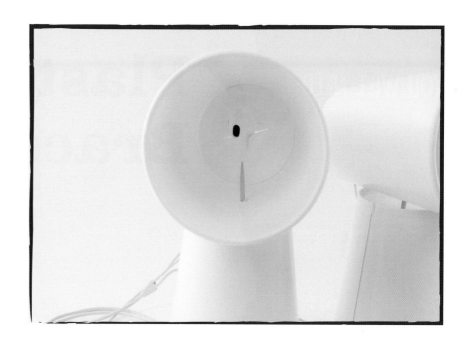

1. Place two cups upside down on the table. Cut a small X in the bottom of each. Then press one ear bud inside each X.

2. Turn the other two cups upside down on the table. Press the pointed end of a toothpick into the paper center at the bottom of each.

3. Now put your hand inside one of these cups and poke the toothpick into the side of a cup with an ear bud in it. Repeat for the other cup. Then turn on the music!

Tip: If you don't have any toothpicks, pull a small paperclip open. Place the paperclip in the cup with the ear bud and press down into the standing cup. The paperclip will hold the cups for each ear bud in place.

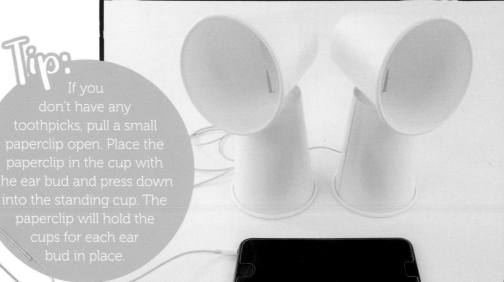

9

Plastic Bag Bracelet

YOU WILL NEED:

- scissors
- plastic grocery bags
- clear tape
- clipboard (optional)

For optional beads:

- glue
- magazines
- pencil

Tip:
You can make a single-color bracelet by using three plastic strips from the same bag. To make a multi-color bracelet, use bags with different colors.

BRAID A PLASTIC BAG BRACELET!

Here's How:

1. Wash and dry the plastic bags. Now transform the plastic bag into yarn you can braid.

2. First, flatten the bag and cut the top handles off.

3. Then cut across the bottom of the bag. After you cut away the top and the bottom of the bag, all that will be left is a wide plastic loop.

4. Smooth out the plastic. Cut three long strips of plastic to the same width.

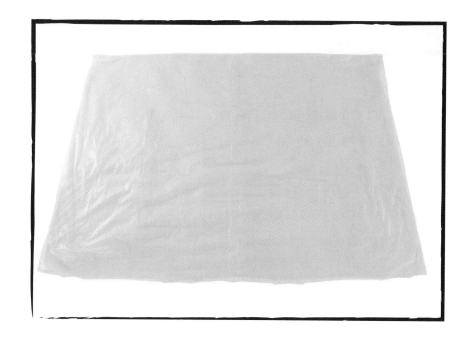

Tip:
Plastic bag yarn is also called **plarn**.

5. Twist each strip to make it round like yarn.

6. Hold all three strips in your hand. Make a knot at one end.

7. Then begin braiding. Continue until you reach the other end. Then make a knot.

8. Tie the two ends of the braid together. Trim the loose edges with the scissors.

Tip: Use a clipboard or clear tape to hold your yarn in place while you twist it and braid it.

HOW TO BRAID

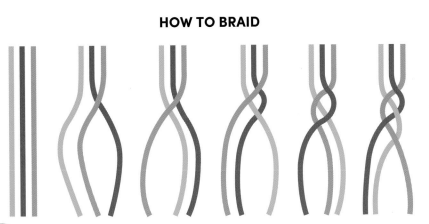

Bonus! Add Beads

You can recycle old magazines to make paper beads for your bracelet. Cut the colorful pages into long triangles with wide bottoms and narrow points at the top.

Wrap the wide end of the triangle around a pencil. Twist the paper around the pencil until only the narrow tip is left. Then add a drop of glue to the tip of the triangle and press it down. After the glue dries, slide the bead off the pencil.

Add the paper beads to the middle strip as you braid your bracelet.

CD Photo Cube

- 4 plastic CD cases (standard size)

- scissors

- pencil

- ruler

- photos or decorative paper

- tracing paper (optional)

- markers (optional)

For optional lamp cube:

- tissue paper

- LED tea light

- washi tape

MAKE A PHOTO CUBE WITH CD CASES!

Here's How:

1. Open all four plastic CD cases and remove the paper inserts.

2. Measure the front insert and use the measurements to create your own artwork with photos, decorative paper, and/or drawings.

3. After you create your artwork, cut the images to size.

Tip:
You can also use large photos inside each wall of the cube without any decorative paper. Before you cut your photo, cut a sheet of tracing paper to the correct size. Place the tracing paper over the photo to help you decide how to **crop** the photo and cut it down to size.

4. Once your art is ready, it's time to assemble your cube. Carefully open each CD case and unclick the front from the back.

5. Flip one side of the CD case over and reconnect the hinges to make a **right angle**. Stand the case up on the table. Repeat for the other three cases.

6. Put your artwork inside one case on the thin CD wall. Then flip another CD case over and place the thick CD wall over the back of your art work.

7. The two cases now form a U shape. Click the thick and the thin CD walls together to hold your art in place. Repeat until all four cases are joined.

flipped

Tip:
The secret to making your cube is to flip the CD case over each time you make a new connection. Then a thick wall will always end up facing a thin wall and you can click them together without any glue.

Bonus! Make a Lamp Cube

You can make your CD cube into a lamp by placing a small LED tea light inside. Use colored tissue paper inside the CD cases to make your lamp glow brightly at night. Cover the top edges of the CD cases with patterned washi tape.

Keyboard Letter Frame

YOU WILL NEED:

- old keyboard

- flathead screwdriver

- small picture frame

- hot glue gun (adult permission)

- newspaper or cardboard (optional)

For optional keyboard word art:

- decorative paper

- stick-on letters

- spray paint

DECORATE A PICTURE FRAME WITH KEYBOARD LETTERS!

Here's How:

1. Unplug the old keyboard or laptop you are going to upcycle.

2. Press the tip of a small flathead screwdriver under a key.

3. Pull the handle of the screwdriver up to pull the key up and out of the keyboard. Repeat until you have removed all of the keys.

4. Wash and dry the keys.

Tip: Some keyboards use plastic retainers or metal springs and bars to hold the key caps in place. You may also need to press the key to the side to release it from the keyboard.

5. Plan your keyboard design. Place the keys along the edges of the picture frame to determine how many rows of keys will fit.

6. Do you want to place all of the letters at the top? Or will you alternate the keys and place some upside down? Move the keys around and see what you like.

7. Prepare the old picture frame for gluing. Remove the backing and the glass.

Tip:

If you don't like the color of the frame, you can use spray paint to change the color. Ask an adult to help you. Paint the frame over newspaper or cardboard in a well-ventilated area.

8. Use the hot glue gun to attach the keyboard letters to the frame. Be careful: hot glue guns can burn you. Make sure you have an adult's help or permission for this.

9. Clean the glass and put it back into the frame.

10. Add a photo or paper with a saying you like. Then close the back.

Tip:

Reassemble the picture frame in a clean area. The glass will attract tiny bits of dust and paper from your work area that you won't notice until you close everything up.

Bonus! Keyboard Word Art

Reverse the process and place the keyboard letters inside the frame as art. Spell a simple word inside a small frame. Glue the letters to decorative paper.

If you need to use a consonant or a vowel more than once to spell the words you want to write, you can upcycle your keyboard letters a different way. After you wash and dry the keys, spray paint all of the keys a new color. The next day, use stick-on letters to write the words you want. Then glue the painted keys to a decorative background and frame your saying.

Tip:
Do you have an old picture frame without any glass? You won't need the glass to make keyboard word art. The keyboard letters will pop out beyond the frame in this 3-D art project.

You can also use the keys to make a monogram, the first initial of someone's last name. Make a paper template first to help you plan where you will glue the keys. Then trace the monogram letter onto the sheet of paper you will use for the background inside the frame. Glue the keys down one by one to form the letter.

YOU WILL NEED:

- CD
- plastic spoons
- paper
- pencil
- scissors
- safety goggles
- glue stick
- hot glue gun (adult permission)
- LED tea light

For optional flower bud:

- small glass jar

24

USE AN OLD CD AND PLASTIC SPOONS TO MAKE A SHINY FLOWER LIGHT!

Here's How:

1. Wash and dry the old plastic spoons.

2. Plan your design before you start cutting and gluing. Place the tea light on the sheet of paper. Draw a pencil line around the edge. Cut out the small paper circle.

3. Rub a glue stick around the clear edge near the hole in the center of the CD. Then place the paper circle over the hole in the CD and center it.

4. Add eight plastic spoons around the edges of the CD. Point the handles toward the center. How much of the handle will you need to cut?

5. Use scissors to cut the handles off the plastic spoons.

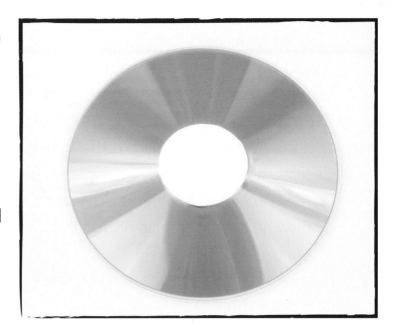

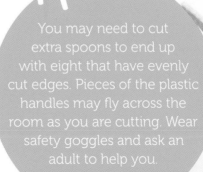

Tip:
You may need to cut extra spoons to end up with eight that have evenly cut edges. Pieces of the plastic handles may fly across the room as you are cutting. Wear safety goggles and ask an adult to help you.

6. One by one, add hot glue to the round bottom of each spoon. Then turn the spoon over and hold it on the CD until it dries in place. Glue all eight spoons to the CD to make the flower design. Be careful: hot glue guns can burn you. Make sure you have an adult's help or permission for this.

7. Remove the paper circle from the center of the CD.

8. Turn on the tea light and place it in the center of the CD.

Tip:

For this flower design, the bowl of the spoon faces up. That means you add the glue under the round bottom of the spoon. Count to five as the hot glue dries.

Bonus! Make a Flower Bud

The flower on your CD is fully open. If you use a small glass jar as the base, you can make a flower bud! Remove the label as you wash the jar in soapy water. Wash and dry more spoons, too. You'll need a lot more of them to make a bigger flower.

How many spoons you will need depends on how tall and wide the glass is. You may need three or even four dozen spoons to make one flower bud.

Tip:

A short drinking glass can also be used. If your glass container has a wide mouth, you may be able to place a tea light inside the flower bud.

After you cut the spoons, figure out where the first row will go. Place one spoon on the glass jar. Turn the spoon so the round bottom faces you and the flat edge touches the glass. Hold the spoon up to the glass so the upper half of the spoon is above the top of the glass. This time the hot glue will go at the bottom of the spoon where you cut off the handle.

Add the hot glue to the handle and glue the first spoon to the glass. Then add a new spoon next to the first one. Glue the second spoon to the glass right next to the first one. Place the two spoons side by side. Continue and make the first row around the glass.

Work your way down to the bottom of the glass, gluing one row at a time. **Stagger** each row so the point of the spoon is centered in the open space of the row above it. As you hold the spoons in each new row next to the glass, pull each spoon flower petal back a bit so it faces outward.

Depending on the height of the jar, you may need three or four rows of flower petal spoons. For the bottom layer of petals, cut off the spoon handles. (You don't want the sharp handles to scratch the table.) After all of the glue dries, place your flower bud in the center of the table and enjoy!

Tip:
You can also paint your spoons or color them with permanent markers before you glue them.

Glossary

crop (KROP): to cut off or remove the tops or edges of something

dimensions (duh-MEN-shuhns): the length, width, and height of an object

plarn (pluh-ARN): yarn made from plastic bags

right angle (RITE ANG-guhl): a 90 degree angle formed when two lines are perpendicular to each other

stagger (STAG-ur): to arrange things in a series of different positions

upcycle (up-SYE-kuhl): to reuse old items and make them into something better

Index

braid 5, 11, 12, 13

CD 5, 24, 25, 26, 27

CD case 5, 14, 15, 16, 17

paint 8, 20, 22, 29

paper cups 5, 6, 7, 8, 9

paper tube 8

plastic bags 10, 11

tape 8, 12, 17

Show What You Know

1. Why do you use two toothpicks or paperclips to build the four cup speakers?
2. How can clear tape or a clipboard help you make your bracelet?
3. What is the secret to making a photo cube stay together without any glue?
4. When would you need to use stick-on letters for your keyboard art?
5. Why should you wear safety goggles while cutting the plastic spoons?

Further Reading

Bolte, Mari, *Eco Gifts: Upcycled Gifts You Can Make*, Capstone Press, 2017.

Donovan, Sandy, *Thrift Shopping: Discovering Bargains and Hidden Treasures*, Twenty-First Century Books, 2015.

Rau, Dana Meachen Rau, *Crafting with Recyclables: Even More Projects*, Cherry Lake Publishing, 2017.

About the Author

Anastasia Suen is the author of more than 300 books for young readers, including *Wired* (A Chicago Public Library Best of the Best Book) about how electricity flows from the power plant to your house. She reads, writes, and edits books in her studio in Northern California.

Meet The Author!
www.meetREMauthors.com

© 2019 Rourke Educational Media

www.rourkeeducationalmedia.com

PHOTO CREDITS: Cover & all pages: © creativelytara

Edited by: Keli Sipperley
Cover and Interior design by: Tara Raymo • CreativelyTara • www.creativelytara.com

Library of Congress PCN Data

Upcycled Gifts and Gadgets / Anastasia Suen
(Make It!)
ISBN 978-1-64156-443-4 (hard cover)
ISBN 978-1-64156-569-1 (soft cover)
ISBN 978-1-64156-688-9 (e-Book)
Library of Congress Control Number: 2018930471

Rourke Educational Media
Printed in the United States of America,
North Mankato, Minnesota